July 18 – 1975

Be[...]

With best wishes —

Earl Mayo

A PARABLE FOR PARENTS AND OTHERS

MR. ADAMS

A PARABLE FOR PARENTS AND OTHERS

CARL MAYS

BROADMAN PRESS · NASHVILLE, TENN.

**Dedicated
to
my wife, Jean
and
my son, Carl, II . . .**

**We
are a young family
still
growing in Christ . . .
Living
Loving
Laughing
Crying . . .
making mistakes—making right decisions
and
thanking God
for
the opportunity
to
do so**

Foreword

When asked to write a foreword to this book, I immediately accepted the opportunity to expand upon the story I had written. Having completed the proposed foreword, however, I was not at all pleased with it. I discarded the initial attempt and tried again. The second endeavor also failed. Like the first, it weakly echoed what had already been said more strongly in the story through the dialogue of Mr. Adams and David Porter and through the recorded thoughts of David.

Then, as I considered another approach to an appropriate introduction, something quickly came to mind—something which had strangely grabbed hold of me when I first encountered it as a high school student. The more I considered these words of William Wordsworth, the more I determined they would be the perfect prologue—and epilogue—to MR. ADAMS: A PARABLE FOR

PARENTS AND OTHERS . . .

My heart leaps up when I behold
        a rainbow in the sky.
So was it when my life began;
So is it now I am a man;
So be it when I shall grow old,
        or let me die!
The child is father of the man;
And I could wish my days to be
Bound each to each by natural piety.

Carl Mays
Gatlinburg, Tennessee

Chapter One

In a way, this story is about me, David Porter. But mostly, it's about Mr. Adams. He's dead now. He died several years ago when I was only ten. His funeral was the first one I ever attended. I'll never forget it—just as I'll never forget him.

A lot of people couldn't understand why Mr. Adams and I were such good friends. I don't know exactly why we were. Maybe it was because we were so much alike. I don't mean we resembled each other physically. He was a seventy-eight-year-old man with wrinkled skin and thin, white hair. What I mean is, we were alike in the way we thought and talked and wondered about things. Also, we both seemed to mess up a lot.

Those are not the only reasons Mr. Adams was my best friend, though. It was more than just because of that. It's sort of hard to explain, but— well, take the day I brought home that terrible report card. Actually, I don't guess any of my report cards could be called great, but this one was worse than usual. I almost failed math.

It really upset my parents. Mr. Adams made me feel better, though, after Mom and Dad jumped all over me. He said, "The worth of a person isn't determined by whether or not he makes an 'A' in math." Now you see why I liked Mr. Adams so much? He was always saying something like that. And, I don't know if what Mr. Adams said had anything to do with it or not, but my math grades began to get better after he talked with me like he did.

Of course, my parents never did seem to like Mr. Adams as much as I did.

He didn't care too much for math or things like that, but he really did like words. He read a lot and shared some of the words with me. To tell the truth, I don't imagine I would be able to write all of this today if it weren't for his help back then. Oh sure, I've had help from teachers since then, but it was Mr. Adams who really set me on the right track.

If you notice as you read, you'll find most of my sentences are complete. I usually include a subject and a verb. My commas, periods, and other types of punctuation are pretty good, too. Mr.

Adams said this is important—to write and to express yourself so people can understand what you are trying to tell them. When I entered high school, my freshman composition instructor called me a welcome relief to what he's getting these days. (Of course, I thought of Mr. Adams and smiled to myself when the instructor said that!)

Getting back to my parents, though, Dad didn't much go for the way Mr. Adams seemed to always take my side in things. What Dad didn't understand, though, is that Mr. Adams did not always agree with me. He disagreed quite a bit. *The way he disagreed, though, was better than most people's agreement.* That's the way Mr. Adams was.

I remember the Christmas when I was supposed to be an angel in the church pageant. It didn't seem so bad when I first told them I would do it. "Heck," I thought, "it might be fun to be a star in a drama." However, as Christmas got closer and the pageant drew nearer, things didn't look so good.

"I don't want to be in the pageant," I told my mother one afternoon, about three days before the drama was to be staged.

We were in the kitchen when I informed her of my decision. She turned around so fast to face me she almost dropped the bowl she was holding. I didn't like the way her eyes looked—not at all.

"You don't want to *what?*" she asked.

"To be in the pageant."

"Well, you certainly *are* going to be in it!"

"Why?" I asked.

"Why? Because you've already told everybody you would do it! Because you've been practicing for it! Because I have made your costume for it!"

"But . . ."

"No 'buts' about it," she interrupted. "You're going to be in the Christmas pageant and that's final!" She paused to catch her breath. "Now go do your math homework. We'll be ready to eat shortly."

My dad felt the same way, he said. I didn't believe he really cared all that much, though. I thought he just went along with my mother at times, to cut down on arguments and stuff.

Well, anyway, I went over to talk to Mr. Adams about the pageant and the angel business. He lived right next door to us. I always thought that was one reason my parents talked about him and didn't entirely approve of our friendship. They seemed to think he was a moocher, because he stayed with his daughter and her husband. It seemed to me his daughter sometimes acted as if she thought the same thing.

"Why don't you want to be in the pageant?"

he asked me. Good ole Mr. Adams! That's why I liked him. Nobody else bothered to ask me why I didn't want to be in it. And, to beat all, *he really wanted to know.* Around him, I just about always got to finish my sentences without an interruption.

"Because some of the guys at school teased me about it," I answered his question.

"I see," Mr. Adams replied. "What did they say?"

"They said angels were sissies." I looked at him. I knew he was listening and thinking about what I said.

"How do you feel about it?" he asked.

"Sir?"

"Do you think angels are sissies?"

"I don't know," I replied. "I guess so, though. They do wear dresses."

"How do you know they wear dresses?"

"That's what my mother made me for the pageant—a long, white dress." I paused for a moment. No one spoke. "I've seen pictures, too," I added.

"You've actually seen *drawings* or *paintings,* haven't you? I don't believe anyone with a camera has ever taken a *picture* of an angel." I listened as he continued. "People don't really know what angels look like. Artists have just drawn ideas of how they imagine them to be."

"Do you think angels look like the drawings

people have made?" I asked him.

"I don't know," he said, "but I certainly don't think angels are sissies." He looked me solidly in the eyes. "Do you realize angels are mentioned approximately three hundred times in the Bible?" I shook my head. "And, do you realize angels are never referred to as females?"

"Really?"

"That's right," Mr. Adams assured me. "Angels such as Michael and Gabriel are described as being strong, powerful figures."

Everything was silent as I considered what Mr. Adams told me.

"Then, why do people think angels wear dresses?" I finally asked.

"Well," Mr. Adams explained, "those are not really dresses. The Bible tells us angels are clothed in *white garments*. Artists have drawn them to wear white robes." He eyed me carefully. "Of course, Samson, the strongest man who ever lived, wore a robe. It was the custom in those days, just like it is the custom today to wear other types of clothing."

My parents were shocked when I appeared anxious to participate in the pageant. My friends at school were surprised to learn of my newly acquired knowledge of angels, too. The clincher came when

I showed them the place in the Bible where an angel actually *wrestled* with Jacob. Mr. Adams pointed this out to me.

Are you beginning to better understand about Mr. Adams now? He took time to talk to a guy about things. He wasn't always saying, "We'll talk about it later," or, "Not now, can't you see I'm busy?" That's something I could never understand when I was a little kid. I couldn't see how reading a newspaper or watching television or something like that could be considered "being busy."

Mr. Adams came to see me in the pageant. After it was over, he told me I was the brightest, strongest-looking angel in the whole church. Boy, that made me feel good—because I knew he meant it. My parents just looked at each other sort of funny-like when he told me that. They didn't understand Mr. Adams. Of course, they didn't understand angels, either.

Chapter Two

Because of his help and because I liked him so much anyway, I wanted to get Mr. Adams something special that Christmas I was in the pageant. When I scraped all my money together, it totaled up to one dollar and forty-five cents. Of course, I wanted to buy something for my mother and father, too. Straining to use the math I hated, I figured I had forty-six and one-third cents to spend on each one of the three. With these financial resources, I headed to the nearest five and dime store.

"Yes sir," the woman addressed me as I walked through the door and down one of the aisles, "what can I do for you?"

"I'd like to see the merchandise you have that costs about forty-five cents," I told her.

Together, we inspected pot holders, vases, pictures, brushes, stationery, ball point pens, and several other items. I wound up getting my mother a big bar of pink soap carved in the shape of a swan. I chose a paper clip holder for my father. I couldn't find anything that I thought would suit Mr. Adams, however, so I decided to look elsewhere. I paid the cashier for the two gifts I purchased. The bill ran to one dollar and four cents, so I had forty-one cents remaining. With this, I journeyed to a discount department store.

I looked at ties, change purses, flashlights, candy, books, and a few other things priced at around forty cents. Then, I saw it. A brilliant idea popped into my mind as I reached up and grasped the red, felt-tipped pen. It was on sale for thirty-nine cents, tax included.

I inserted my remaining two pennies into a gumball machine as I exited through the department store door. Chewing the gum, I pulled up my coat collar to shield my neck from the cold December wind. I was happy. It was the day before Christmas Eve and I had the perfect gift for Mr. Adams. At least, I had it in my mind.

Arriving home, I rushed to my room. Once inside the doorway, I hesitated for a moment. I turned all my energies to trying to remember where I had placed the green construction paper. Mr. Adams had often told me I was destined to be a poet.

That's why he declared I didn't need to be a whiz at math.

"You can hire a secretary to do your figuring for you," he informed me. "You have a way with words," he said, "and words are more important than numbers."

"In the closet," I told myself. "I think I stacked the paper in the closet." Sure enough, it was where I thought it was, neatly stored away on the second shelf from the floor. It was about the only neat thing around, though, according to my mother. At the time, it seemed to me that she revealed to everyone that I must be the messiest kid in the world.

"A straight mind," Mr. Adams told my mother. "That son of yours has a straight mind. It's unbcluttered and it's going to do great things." My mother smiled weakly when he shared this idea with her.

"He can't even keep a straight room," she replied.

I pulled the paper from the shelf and spread a couple of pieces on the floor. On one piece, which was torn and a little ragged around the edges, I stroked a line with the red, felt-tipped pen. "Perfect!" I exclaimed inwardly. "The red on green will make a perfect Christmas card. Now to come up with a perfect poem!"

Many thoughts went through my mind. I began

several lines of poetry that evening. Some I erased. Some I kept. I wanted to be sure it was just right before I made my final copy with red on green.

I didn't complete the poem before bedtime, but stored what I had, ready to finish it the next day, Christmas Eve. Sleep didn't come quickly. Instead, lines of poetry continued to flood my brain. A couple of times during the night, I arose from bed to jot down some ideas.

The next morning I continued to labor with my enjoyable task. Morning became afternoon. Finally, at about three o'clock, I made my last draft. After transferring it to the green paper, I carefully wrapped the homemade card and ran over to Mr. Adams' house.

Mr. Adams looked sort of sad and lonely when he answered the door. He was alone. "The others are doing some last minute shopping," he said. I had overheard my mother and Mr. Adams' daughter discussing his physical condition. I knew he had been a little sick. This was the first time I noticed it in his eyes, though.

"Merry Christmas, Mr. Adams!" I handed him the Christmas card wrapped in white paper and tied with a red ribbon.

His eyes brightened and lost some of their glossy redness. The blue veins in his hand looked hard, pressing against his skin as he received the gift. "Thank you, David," he said softly. He slowly walked over to a table near the bright Christmas tree. He picked up a small package wrapped in multi-colored paper and tied with purple ribbon. He turned to face me again. A big grin stretched across his thin lips as he extended the present toward me. "And Merry Christmas to you," he smiled.

I reached out to accept what I knew would always be a prized possession. It was small and flat. "Can I open it now?" I asked.

He nodded his head slightly. "If I can open mine," he replied.

"Yes sir," I answered, "but be careful—you might tear what's inside."

We both began unwrapping our surprises.

Sitting on a nearby sofa, he heeded my warning. Ever so nimbly, he untied the bow and pulled at the paper. Working faster and too excited to sit, I interrupted his endeavors.

"A book!" I exclaimed as I tore into the wrapping.

"Yes," he said, looking up, "a very special book."

I removed the small, thin book from the remaining paper. I turned it over. "A dictionary!"

"It'll fit in your back pocket," Mr. Adams told

me. "You can carry it with you all the time."

He knew I liked it. He could tell by the expression on my face. I didn't have to say anything. I did, though. I told him how much I appreciated it and I promised to learn a new word every day. He really liked that idea and I was happy it pleased him.

"Open yours," I said.

Once again, he resumed his cautious unveiling. Finally, he reached the green card inscribed with red ink. He studied the picture of the angel I had drawn on the front. The angel was muscular. At the same time, he had an expression of kindness about him. I knew it wasn't the best drawing in the world, but I was proud of it. Mr. Adams was proud of it, too. He told me so.

Then, he opened the card and silently began to read the poem I had written. Watching him, I beamed.

It took him longer to read the poem than I thought it would. Usually, he was a fast reader.

Mr. Adams' eyes became moist. He looked up at me. "This is the best poem I have ever read," he said. I stood still, surprised, because I knew he had read many poems. "And it's the nicest gift I have ever received," he continued. I didn't know what to say.

"Really?" I managed to mutter.

"Really," he assured me.

I felt taller than I ever felt in my life when I walked home from Mr. Adams' house that afternoon. My parents didn't have to get onto me or fuss at me for anything the rest of the day. I guess they thought I was just trying to be good because it was Christmas Eve. They didn't know I had already experienced the best Christmas a person could possibly have.

Chapter Three

Mr. Adams made me feel good lots of times. That Christmas was something special, but he seemed to have a habit of making me happy all through the year. He helped me to like myself. *He made me glad I am me.* This may sound odd, but that's what he did. For example, one day we were talking about God and the Bible. Mr. Adams enjoyed doing that—talking about God and the Bible. "Thou shalt love thy neighbor as thyself," he read.

"What if a person doesn't love himself?" I asked.

"Then he would have trouble loving others," he quickly replied. He stared at me. "Do you love yourself?" he asked. "Do you like yourself?"

"I guess so," I answered. "Sometimes it's hard, though."

"Many people go through life not loving themselves—or even liking themselves," Mr. Adams informed me. "Because of this lack of self-love and self-esteem, these people destroy their talents, energies, and creative abilities."

I didn't always understand everything Mr. Adams said. However, I usually understood enough to get an idea of what he was talking about. I know he helped me to like myself and to love myself more. The times when I was just about ready to give up on something, Mr. Adams would come through to save the day. Like the time I tried out for the baseball team.

"He's going to try out for the baseball squad," my father told my mother as he nodded toward me at the dinner table.

"Well, I hope you don't trip on a blade of grass and break an arm or something," she said.

She was kidding, of course. At least, looking back on it, I think she was kidding. However, people usually mean something by it when they kid that way. At the time, I didn't really know how to take her. Only a few days earlier, I had overheard her tell some of her friends I was accident-prone. I mean, she's always been a good mother and everything, but when she said things like that, it sure didn't help a guy love himself. Know what I mean?

My father was a little better at encouraging me to do things. Somehow, though, he always seemed to think I wasn't as tough and manly as he was when he was a boy. He was always telling me about something he did when he was nine or ten. If he wasn't telling me directly, he was telling my mother and making sure I overheard him.

"Kids today have it too soft," I heard him say many times. I don't know. Maybe I did have it too soft when I was a little kid. That's the only time I'll ever be a kid, though, so I'll never know any different.

Well, anyway, getting back to the baseball deal: my parents didn't help me believe I could make the team. Oh sure, they wanted me to get on it, but I could tell they didn't have much confidence in me. That's where Mr. Adams came through again.

"Feelings of inferiority are among the most common symptoms of self-hate," is what he told me. Then, seeing that I didn't understand him, he went on to explain to me what he meant. He explained that I mustn't build up the talents of other people in my mind and belittle my own talents. He said it was bad to exaggerate others' while underestimating myself.

"You are more capable of being a good baseball player than you think," he told me.

By the time I left Mr. Adams' house that day, I almost believed I could make first team for the

New York Yankees! And you know what? I did earn a spot on the local squad. Sure, I struck out some and made a few errors. But, as Mr. Adams said, "Who doesn't?" He told me himself he saw Babe Ruth strike out and drop some fly balls.

Of course, I practiced. Mr. Adams stressed the importance of planning for things. "Don't take anything for granted," he warned me. "Believe you can do it and then work to prove you can."

That's why he gave me the dictionary for Christmas. I told him I would like to be a writer and write books like the ones he read.

"If you're going to be a ditch digger," he said, "you've got to learn how to use a shovel. There's a technique to it. Some people can dig a ditch in a couple of hours. Some people couldn't dig one in two days." He paused and squinted his eyes as he looked into mine. "If you want to be a writer, you've got to learn how to use words. Some people can express themselves in two words. Some people can't express themselves in two hundred words."

Man, Mr. Adams could sure express himself. He could get through to me when no one else could. Even though this was good, in a way, it was also bad. It sort of made my parents mad when they complained about not being able to communicate with me.

Actually, at the time, I didn't believe my parents cared anything about really communicating with me. And I felt that they didn't want Mr. Adams to be able to, either. Looking back on it, I realize they've always loved me, but as a nine- or ten-year-old kid, I knew my parents didn't understand angels or Mr. Adams and I didn't understand them.

When my baby sister was born, things around the house really got hectic. Right before the baby came, I was just beginning to think I understood my parents a little. Then, bam! The baby came along and I thought my parents acted like they wanted to kick me out of the place . . . sort of like trading an old car for a new one.

"Stay away from the crib," my mother ordered. "Don't get too close to her, you might give her germs. Get that cat out of here! Don't you realize they carry diseases!" It was always something like this. Of course, many of the things she said were probably blown all out of proportion in my mind. Nevertheless, to me, it was all too real.

My mother even seemed to brag to her friends about the number of diapers the baby could dirty. This really caused me to not understand parents. It seemed to me that she would complain to everybody about how messy I was and then brag about the baby's ability to dirty the diapers. "Why, I've just never seen anything like it," she would smile and say to her friends. "That girl can dirty more diapers than any child I have ever seen!"

Mr. Adams laughed when I told him about this. He sympathized with me, though, when I told him how I would go to the bathroom and find dirty diapers in the commode.

"It's easy to love the lovely," Mr. Adams advised me as he laughed a little, "but it's difficult to love the unlovely."

"You mean I'm supposed to love dirty diapers in the commode?" I asked him.

Then, Mr. Adams came out with a statement which took a lot of explaining. He finally got me to understand what he meant, though. At least, I understand now—and I think I understood it then.

"Our individual acts of good or bad mean very little," is what he said. "It is the way we are all the time that is important. It's our moods and attitudes—the way we act and react day-in and day-out."

He went on to tell me I could love the baby without loving the dirty diapers. "You can love a person and hate his ways," Mr. Adams said. "If a mother has a criminal son, she can love him while she hates what he does."

As I mentioned earlier, sometimes Mr. Adams

got kind of deep for a nine- or ten-year-old kid. Like I said, though, I usually understood generally what he meant, even if I couldn't always understand everything. And that's something else I liked about him. He treated me like I was somebody. He didn't think I was lower than him. He didn't ignore me or look over me. He always took time to really talk with me.

It hasn't been so long that I can't remember how good it made me feel to know somebody wanted to talk with me and explain things to me, even though I was only a kid. The more I think about it, the more I miss Mr. Adams. I'm thankful, though, that I had a chance to know him when he was here—at the time I probably needed him most.

Chapter Four

In case you're wondering if I'm the only boy Mr. Adams helped out, I'm not. I was his closest friend, but all the kids in the neighborhood liked him. Even some girls.

"My mother is always trying to trick me into lying to her," Emily Alexander told Mr. Adams.

"What do you mean?" Mr. Adams asked her.

"Well," Emily replied, "she's always asking me questions she already knows the answers to. Then, if I mess up and don't answer them right, she really gets onto me."

Mr. Adams glanced at me and then gave his attention to Emily. "What kind of questions?" he inquired.

"Yesterday she asked me how I was doing in my science course in school. I told her I was doing okay. She said I was lying because she had talked with my teacher who claimed I didn't have my mind on the subject."

"I see," Mr. Adams said.

"She's always doing something like that," Emily added.

"Then, why do you lie?" Mr. Adams asked her. "If you know she's trying to trick you, why don't you tell the truth?"

"I don't know," Emily answered. "I guess it's because I know I'm going to get punished anyway."

"How's that?" Mr. Adams asked again.

"If I told her I was doing poorly in science, she would punish me for it. When I lie, there's always a chance she won't find out about it."

"So you lie because you get punished for telling the truth?"

"Yes sir," Emily Alexander answered.

Mr. Adams was silent for a couple of seconds. He glanced over toward me again, then looked back into Emily's eyes. "Why don't you tell your mother what you told me?" Mr. Adams suggested.

"Oh no," she quickly replied, "I could never do that!"

"Why?"

"Because my mother would get mad and really let me have it. I know she would!" The girl looked at Mr. Adams with wide eyes, then exchanged quick glimpses with me.

I knew how Emily felt. It seemed to be the same way at my house. For example, some of my mother's friends were coming by all the time to see the new baby. "What do you think of your baby sister?" they would ask me. What could I say? There we were—my mother, the friends, the baby, and me. You know what I really thought about the baby—dirty diapers and all. But I couldn't tell my mother's friends that. I knew I had to lie about it. I felt if I told the truth, I would never hear the end of it.

Well, anyway, getting back to Emily Alexander: Mr. Adams helped her just as he did me a lot of times. Somehow, he would relay the troubles we were having to our parents. And most of the time our parents would get mad at him for "sticking his nose" in other people's business. After they got over their madness, though, they would usually realize Mr. Adams was right and you could tell a difference in things.

Of course, we kids really got talked to for discussing our "family matters" with him.

"Some things are family secrets," my mother would say. "They're not for outsiders to hear."

"That's right" my father would support her. "What you kids see in that old man anyway, I'll never understand." He didn't have to tell me that.

I knew he didn't understand.

Not too many adults did understand Mr. Adams—not even Mr. Whitlow, the elderly man who managed the "L & W Supermarket" in our neighborhood. Mr. Adams went to talk with Mr. Whitlow about one of my friends, Cecil Barton. It all came about because Mr. Whitlow thought Cecil broke out one of the supermarket windows.

"I heard the window break and I saw you running away," Mr. Whitlow told Cecil.

"I didn't do it!" Cecil explained.

Mr. Whitlow looked at him very sternly. "If you didn't do it, why did you run?"

"I don't know," Cecil answered, "but I didn't do it. Honest, I didn't!"

"I saw you, son," Mr. Whitlow continued. "You'll have to ask God to make you a better boy. It makes God sad when one of his little children tells a lie."

I knew Cecil didn't break the window. He told Mr. Adams and me he didn't, and I believed him. I knew he ran because he was afraid—just like any kid would be afraid if he was around when a window was broken.

Cecil got a whipping, though. His parents thought he did it; they believed he was lying.

No one seemed to like it too much when Mr. Adams defended Cecil and said he didn't believe

Cecil broke the window. But there were sure a lot of red faces when another kid's parents phoned Mr. Whitlow and told him their boy had confessed to breaking the window.

That's another thing about Mr. Adams. He believed in people. He stood by you, too—no matter what. Even if it seemed everyone else was against you, he still stood up for you.

I'll tell you something he didn't like, though. He didn't like to see "pushy" people. He talked about *hate* disguised as *love*.

"It's not right for someone to impose or push his beliefs on another person, pretending he's doing it for the other person's own good," he told me. The reason he said this is because Stan Kirkendall and I got into an argument about how something was supposed to be done.

We were going to form a secret club is what we were going to do. I thought it should be a club just for boys only, but Stan said we should allow girls, too, if they could pass the test. I got mad at him when he kept on insisting we ought to let girls join. He got mad at me when I said no.

"Girls are too sissy," I told him.

"Yeah?" he snarled. "You know who the fastest runner in our class is, don't you?"

"They're still sissies," I answered. "Some of them

are fast sissies, but they're still sissies!"

"If our club races another club, we would win every time," he argued.

"We don't have to have any races," I came back. "Besides, girls are too clean!"

"What do you mean?" he snapped.

"Most of them probably take a bath every day," I informed him.

This sort of made him stop and think a little, but he was still too stubborn to realize we shouldn't have girls in the club. So, we went to see Mr. Adams.

"What do you have against girls, David?" he started with me.

"Nothing, Mr. Adams, I just don't think they should be in our secret club—that's all."

He asked some more questions and we told him about the things we had said. After listening to both sides, he thought each of us had some good points.

"Why don't you have *two* clubs?" he finally suggested. Then, he went on to explain how I could be the leader of the all-boys club and Stan could head up the mixed group.

"You both can be members of each club," he continued. "That way, you can try out both ideas." He paused and winked at us. "If they both work out, keep them. If one doesn't work, drop it. If neither works, drop them both—study what went wrong, and start all over again."

That Mr. Adams—man, he was something else!

Chapter Five

Mr. Adams was always challenging me to think. But he said it was important to have the right kind of thoughts. "Thoughts cannot be kept secret," he told me, "no matter how hard you try to keep them secret. They always come to the surface in our everyday lives, showing up in our attitudes, actions, and reactions." Time and time again, I would hear Mr. Adams quote, "As a man thinketh in his heart, so is he."

I guess that's why the bathroom was my favorite room. I could think there. It was the only place in the house where I could go and lock the door and be alone without everyone wondering why the door was shut. I believe I could have stayed in the bathroom for hours if my parents would have let me.

In my own bedroom, if I ever shut the door, someone would poke a head in and say, "What'cha got the door shut for?" Sometimes when this happened, I would be getting dressed, or maybe I had come to my room to finish drying off after taking a bath. Times like this embarrassed me. I realized my parents saw me naked when I was a baby, but still, I sure didn't like for them to see me getting dressed or drying off when I was around nine or ten. If I tried to cover up when they barged in, they would just sort of laugh and say, "Don't be silly," or something like that.

Well, anyway, getting back to thinking: it seems I could always do my best thinking in the bathroom or in the mornings when I was putting on my socks. I could usually wake up and brush my teeth and put on my underwear and shirt and pants and everything in just a couple of minutes. But when it came to putting on my socks, I guess it probably took me at least five or ten minutes.

"What'cha doing in there?" my mom would yell from the kitchen to my bedroom.

"Puttin' on my socks."

"Well, it shouldn't take all morning to put on a pair of socks!"

"Yes'm," I'd agree, and then I'd stop thinking and start putting. I seemed to lose a lot of good thoughts that way.

But I could always catch up on my lost thoughts

when Mr. Adams and I had our "thinking sessions." During these sessions, Mr. Adams and I would sit and think together. No television. No reading. No talking. Nothing going on but thinking.

"Thinking helps a person clean up his mind," Mr. Adams would say. "People are concerned with washing their cars and clothes and dishes and faces and hands and bodies and dogs, but tend to overlook giving their minds a good scrubbing." So we would sit together and scrub our minds.

Usually, after we had sat in silence and thought awhile, we'd share our thoughts with each other. It was at times like this that we had some of our best discussions. Of course, the things we talked about got kind of deep at times, and weird, for a kid my age. But even though I didn't completely understand everything that came up, I usually got the general idea. And I enjoyed *real* talking. We didn't just throw a bunch of words at one another, like people often do. We really talked—communicated, I guess you would say.

"Why do people draw pictures when we have cameras?" I asked Mr. Adams one day after a rather lengthy thinking session in his backyard. He was looking up at the fluffy clouds in the blue sky and the tops of the trees, while I was studying the grass and squeezing some of the blades between my fingers.

He glanced over my way, then again stared at the sky and the treetops. "True artists never draw exactly what they see," he said.

"They don't?"

"No."

"Why?"

"They draw more than is visible to the eye."

"Why?"

"Because it is their desire to help people to see things with new insights," Mr. Adams told me.

"New insights?" I asked, trying to understand.

He knew I was puzzled. "To help people to look at things in new ways—in different ways," he explained. "Five artists could paint the same scene, but each of the paintings would be different. They would each interpret the scene differently." He looked at me. "Know what I mean?"

"Yes sir," I nodded my head, "I think so." I did understand what he meant. Not as well as I understand now, but I did understand.

"It's the same in writing," he continued.

"You mean different writers write about the same thing in different ways?" I asked, to make sure I knew what he was talking about. He nodded his head, then turned to look at a fat bird which had just landed on a small limb and was making it vibrate.

"The best example of this is found in the New Testament's four Gospels. Each of the books contains writings about the same general things, but each is written from a different viewpoint."

I thought about what he said as I mashed the grass blades and brushed the sticky results on my pants. Using the word he had used only a few moments before, I said, "The different writers give us different *insights* into the life of Jesus?"

"Correct," Mr. Adams replied. The fat bird flew away and the limb bounced like a spring. Mr. Adams turned toward me once more. "The main purpose of the four Gospels is to point people to faith in Jesus. Various facts are revealed by the writers. Some emphasize some things; others emphasize other things." I was caught up in what he was saying, and he smiled at my attentiveness.

"The Bible has a lot of good stories," I told him.

"Stories, facts, information, history—the Bible has all of these things," he spoke seriously. "But we must never forget that the Bible was not written merely to help us know these stories, facts, information, and history. Primarily, it was written so that we might know God through his Son, Jesus."

"Yes sir," I said, to let him know that I knew. Then I continued, using another of the words he

had just used. "And the *viewpoints* of the different writers can help us to understand better, can't they?"

He smiled at me again, broadly. Reflecting back upon it, I suppose he smiled, at least in part, when he thought of a boy my age discussing such a subject and using such words. "Of course, different viewpoints can sometimes cause problems," he kept up the conversation.

"What do you mean?" I asked.

"One man's *good* is another man's *bad*. One man's *right* is another man's *wrong*. Conflicts arise when one man's *yes* is another man's *no*."

I felt like a barrel of soap had just been poured into my mind and that I would never be able to rinse it out! Mr. Adams saw I was confused, however, and he went on to help me at least get some idea of what he was talking about.

"Always remember, David," he said, "people come from different backgrounds and grow up being exposed to different teachings. So if someone doesn't interpret something—a scene or idea or whatever—exactly like you do, don't automatically think this person has to be wrong." There seemed to be invisible chains linking my eyes to Mr. Adams' eyes. No longer did either of us appear to be aware of the clouds and sky or the trees and grass. "At the same time, David," he continued, "never compromise your beliefs and values just to please another person or group."

I remember thinking, as I was on my way home that afternoon, that Mr. Adams had gotten deeper than he had ever gone before. But that was one of the most important afternoons in my life. "People have great talents for self-delusion," is something else he told me that day. He said, "We can sometimes make our *bad* appear *good,* while making someone else's *good* appear *bad.*"

Well, anyway, Mr. Adams taught me how to be a better thinker. And he helped me to realize how important it is for people to really think. "Beautiful butterflies come from cocoons," is the way he put it. "Giant oak trees come from acorns. Great achievements come from ideas."

It's something to think about, isn't it?

Chapter Six

When I was a kid, I suppose getting mad was one of my worst faults. I still have to work at it to control my temper. The reason I'm telling this is because Mr. Adams said I should. Oh, he didn't exactly come out and say, "Tell everybody you get mad." What he did say is, "It's good for a person to recognize his own faults. It will help you to overcome your faults if you talk about them." So, we talked quite a lot about anger.

"The Bible teaches us that anger can destroy a person," Mr. Adams stressed. He underlined a lot of things in his Bible. You could tell he read and studied it often, because it was almost worn out and had writing all in it. I remember how I used to think how different it looked from the Bible my mother kept on the table in our living room.

"He that is slow to anger is better than the mighty . . . " is one of the sentences underlined in Mr. Adams' Bible.

"It's from *Proverbs,*" he instructed me, "written by King Solomon, the wisest man who ever lived."

"But it's hard not to get mad," I told him.

"What are some things that make you mad?" Mr. Adams asked.

"I don't know," I answered. "You sort of just have to wait until it happens before you know what it is."

He nodded his head, then he spoke. "Can you remember the last time you got mad?"

I thought for a moment. "Yesterday."

"Oh?" he said. "What happened then?"

"We were going to visit some relatives, and mother wanted me to wear a new shirt and a new pair of pants she bought for me."

"And you didn't want to wear them?"

"No."

"Why?"

"Because I don't like to wear new stuff."

"Why not?"

"It's not comfortable. It just doesn't feel good."

"I know what you mean," Mr. Adams said. I was sort of surprised. I didn't know he didn't like to wear new clothes, either.

"Really?" I asked.

"Really," he told me. "New clothes are just not

as comfortable as the old, well-worn ones." He wasn't just putting me on. I could tell he really meant it.

"I sure wish my mother felt that way," I said. "She thinks it's silly not to want to wear new clothes. I told her it might help if she would wash them a few times before I put them on."

"What did she say to that?"

"She looked at me like she thought I was crazy. 'Kids,' she said, 'I'll never understand them!' "

"That's the problem," Mr. Adams murmured, "most people don't try."

"Sir?" I asked.

"Oh, nothing," he answered. "Nothing—I was just talking to myself." He paused. No one said anything. He rocked in his chair and looked out the window.

"Can you recall some other occasions lately when you became angry?" he picked up.

Several instances began to pop into my mind. "Do you like liver and onions?" I asked. "With asparagus and cooked tomatoes?"

He smiled slightly. "Sounds pretty good to me," he answered.

"Well, it sure doesn't sound good to me! As a matter of fact, I hate it—all of it!"

"Some people like some things; some people like

other things," he reasoned. "That's why they make about a dozen different flavors of *Jell-O*."

"My mother thinks I should like everything—even liver and onions and that other junk."

"And that's what makes you mad?"

"When she forces me to either eat it or go to bed hungry, I get mad."

"Does this happen often?"

"It happens everytime we have liver, fish, or something else I can't stand."

Mr. Adams was silent for a couple of seconds. "What do you like to eat?" he asked.

"I like more things than I don't like, but it seems we're always having the stuff I don't like."

Waiting for me to continue, Mr. Adams didn't say anything.

"I like roast beef, hamburgers, and hot dogs best of all the meats," I said. "I like any kind of potatoes—baked, mashed, or fried, especially French fries."

"You're making me hungry just talking about it," Mr. Adams grinned and licked his lips.

"Yeah," I agreed. "Peas, raw carrots, celery, and raw tomatoes are good, too." Just thinking about it, I began to look forward to the next meal.

We exchanged a few more comments about food, and then Mr. Adams explained to me that my mother was proud of me and wanted me to look extra nice when we went to visit our relatives. He also told me how it was a mother's duty to make sure her children received balanced meals. My parents never knew it, but it was because of discussions with Mr. Adams that I began to understand them better.

"What do you do when you get mad?" Mr. Adams asked me one time when we were talking about anger.

"It's according who I get mad at," I answered.

"What do you mean?"

"Well, if I get mad at one of my friends, I might hit him or throw something at him. If it's a girl, I'd probably shoot her with a rubber band or something." He didn't say anything. "I'm usually sorry for it later, though. We usually make up when we cool down."

"What if the person you're mad at is not someone your age?"

"If my parents make me mad, I usually go to my room and think about how mad I am. There's not much else I can do. I can't hit them or shoot them with a rubber band or something.

"Does anyone else make you mad—besides your parents and friends?"

"Sometimes at school a teacher may punish me

when I don't deserve it. Or, she may embarrass me or something. I don't like that."

"What do you do then?"

"I just take it. Nothing else to do. If I talk back or something, I'll really get into trouble." Mr. Adams didn't speak. He expected me to continue.

"Sometimes when my parents or teacher or somebody makes me mad, I think up different ways to get even."

"Revenge?" Mr. Adams asked.

"I guess so," I confessed, "but I never get around to really doing anything. Just thinking about doing it helps, though."

We talked some more about getting mad and how it really tears up a guy inside. "Makes me feel like I'm going to explode sometimes," I told him.

He gave me some suggestions on how to control my temper. "But, when you do get mad," he said, "try always to talk to someone about it. Tell the person you talk with why you're mad, and tell him how it makes you feel. Getting it off your chest will help you feel better. It'll help you calm down inside," he told me.

I asked Mr. Adams if I could talk with him when I got mad. He said I could. He also suggested I should talk with my parents sometime or with some of my friends. He even told me it would help if

I talked with my dog. And it did.

"I don't care about choosing new clothes," I told my dog one day, "but with new shoes it's different."

He didn't say anything, of course. He just sort of cocked his head to one side and looked at me.

"I like new shoes," I said, "but only if I can pick them out by myself. My mother doesn't think I have enough sense to know what I want!" I was almost crying.

He barked.

"Why can't a guy pick out his own shoes?"

He barked again.

"A guy should at least have that right!"

He barked again, wagged his tail, and jumped on me. I don't know if he was agreeing or disagreeing with me. That's one good thing about talking to a dog, though—you can always decide for yourself what he's saying.

Chapter Seven

Talking about animals, there was this seven-year-old kid who lived down the block from me. He treated animals terrible. Craig Spencer was always tying a string around some cat's neck and swinging the cat around in a circle or hanging it from a tree. And he was always thumping cats on their noses with his finger. He really got a big kick out of thumping cats.

"You can tell a lot about a person by the way he treats animals," Mr. Adams used to say. I sure understood what Mr. Adams meant when he said that, and I agreed with him. I never did care for cats all that much when I was a little kid—dogs have always been my favorites—but it sure burned me to see some guy picking on a cat just for the fun of it.

One of the worst things I ever heard of, though, happened to this new girl who moved into our neighborhood shortly before Mr. Adams died. All of us other kids thought her father was a celebrity. He worked at Disneyland in California before the family moved to our town.

Well, anyway, the girl had a lamb one time when she lived on a farm. Her father was a farmer before he worked at Disneyland. Elizabeth Carter is her name and she had to give away her lamb when they moved from the country to the city. She didn't want to give up the lamb, but her parents finally persuaded her to leave it with some friends.

A couple of years passed and the lamb became a sheep and everybody just seemed to forget what had been a terrible episode in Elizabeth's life. Then, these same friends invited Elizabeth and her parents to come back out to the country and take part in a "dinner-on-the-grounds" reunion at their church's homecoming celebration.

All the way out to the country, Elizabeth thought about seeing her pet lamb who had now grown up, and she asked her parents if they thought the lamb would remember her, and they said they didn't know. Her excitement grew as they neared their friends' home.

This delightful excitement turned into a tragic experience upon the family's arrival and upon the discovery that Elizabeth's lamb had become a barbecued delicacy for dinner. At first, Elizabeth couldn't believe it. Then, when she saw her pet lamb hanging over the barbecue pit, she started crying, became hysterical, began throwing up, and turned the celebration into a disaster.

Can you imagine it—being invited to dinner and discovering the main course is your pet? Mr. Adams just couldn't get over it when Elizabeth told us about it. And she had been in our neighborhood only a short time before Mr. Adams saw to it she got a dog.

"Can you really get me a dog?" she inquired of Mr. Adams when he asked her if she would like to have one.

"Sure," Mr. Adams replied. "I have a friend at the animal shelter who can let you pick out the one you want."

That's how I got my dog—through Mr. Adams' friend.

"I don't know," my mother said when I told her about my desire to have a dog.

"Dogs are a lot of trouble," my father added.

"I'd probably end up having to feed him and take care of him," my mother came back.

"No, I'm afraid it's out of the question now," my father continued. "We don't have enough room."

Things worked out, though. I got the dog. And when my parents agreed to let me have one, I told Mr. Adams, "Mom and Dad aren't too good on this day-in and day-out stuff you talked about, but every now and then they come up with something good."

"They love you," Mr. Adams said, "but it's difficult being parents during this day and time."

As I reflect upon it now, I'm sure my parents treated me better than I thought they were treating me, and they probably liked and understood Mr. Adams more than I thought they did. However, at the time, things didn't seem that way. As an eight- or nine- or ten-year-old, it seemed to me that Mom sometimes would prepare liver and onions and asparagus just because she knew I didn't like it.

Well, anyway, the dog I got was a big, gray, floppy-eared hound with a sad face. I named him *Smoky,* because he was the color of smoke. I could tell Smoky was meant to belong to me because he started messing up and getting into trouble right off the bat.

"We ought to make old man Adams take him off our hands," I heard my father tell my mother. "He's the one who got us into all of this."

They were upset because the neighbors com-

plained about Smoky. One woman threatened to call the police if Smoky didn't stop howling at sirens. "My husband works at night," she said, "and he can't sleep during the day if that blasted dog keeps up that infernal noise!"

However, with the help of Mr. Adams and a switch, I finally broke Smoky of the habit of howling. Smoky liked children, though—especially little children. This didn't help matters any. The mother a couple of doors down got all excited when Smoky was around. She had two children—a two-year-old girl and a three-year-old boy. Smoky liked them very much. And Smoky licked people he liked. The mother didn't seem to appreciate this show of affection. So, she also threatened to call the police if Smoky didn't stay out of her yard and away from her children.

So, we got a long chain and hooked it onto the clothesline in our backyard. This was Mr. Adams' suggestion and it worked pretty good—for awhile—until Smoky pulled down the clothesline. But even this would not have been so bad if my mother had not had some sheets and a white bedspread hanging on the line.

After that, Mr. Adams and I fastened Smoky to a tree and Mr. Adams assured me it would work. It did, too—a lot better than the clothesline deal.

"If at first you don't succeed, try, try again," Mr. Adams would say.

"Of all the places in the world for him to live, why does it have to be next door to us?" I heard my mother ask my father.

Well, anyway, the new girl on the block, Elizabeth, got her dog. She named him *Major*. Major, like Smoky, seemed to have a talent for getting into trouble. The neighbors complained again and blamed Mr. Adams for bringing another *mutt* into the neighborhood. I remember thinking, "It's sure strange how you can make so many people unhappy by trying to make somebody happy."

"At least we can be thankful Adams just lives next door to us, instead of *with* us!" my father told my mother. They went on to discuss the problem Mr. Adams' daughter and her husband had because Mr. Adams lived with them. As I overheard my parents talk, I thought how great it would be if Mr. Adams did live with us.

I liked to go over to Mr. Adams' room. It was different from the rest of the house. It was a lot neater and everything was always in order. I didn't care too much about my room being neat, but I thought Mr. Adams' room wouldn't look right if something wasn't where it was supposed to be.

In the room he had a bookcase full of books,

a desk, and the usual things such as a bed, chest of drawers, closet, and items like that. He had an old rocking chair, too. It was in front of the window where he did most of his reading.

I really enjoyed looking at the pictures on his walls. My favorite was a picture of a herd of wild horses thundering across the prairie and stomping up swirls of dust. I remember how real I thought their flared nostrils looked as they ran.

Mr. Adams always kept his arrowheads displayed on the bookcase and chest of drawers. He had the largest arrowhead collection I'd ever seen. Now it's mine. The picture of the horses is mine, too, along with the underlined, worn-out Bible.

"I'll die one of these days," Mr. Adams told me, "and I want you to have the picture and the collection." He looked at me and paused a couple of seconds before he continued. "They're to look at. My Bible will be yours, also—if you'll promise to do more than just look at it."

I didn't like to hear Mr. Adams talk about dying. I realized, however, that he wasn't afraid to die. He called it, "Going home to be with God."

"It is appointed unto man once to die," Mr. Adams quoted from the Bible. "We ought to make the most of life while we have it," he stressed. "Live a full life on earth and show love for God, your fellow man, and yourself," is the way he instructed me.

"What's heaven like?" I asked Mr. Adams one day.

Mr. Adams looked out his window and rocked very slowly in the old rocking chair. "A lot of people have many different ideas about heaven," he said. He kept on rocking and seemed to be in deep thought. I waited for him to speak again.

"Before a baby comes into this world, he is inside his mother's body. There, he is fairly safe. His needs are met. However, when the baby is born, a whole new existence begins. His capacity for living is multiplied tremendously." He turned his eyes from the window and focused them upon me.

"I think that's what heaven is like, David. Here, on earth, we are living, walking, talking, thinking, acting, and reacting. We strive to live life to the fullest. However, I believe when a person dies and exits this earthly existence, it is like being born again—born into a new world which offers a much greater capacity for living." He paused, then began to rock slowly again. He gazed through the window, appearing to look upward, toward the sky. "Yes, David," he said, "dying and going to heaven is comparable to leaving a mother's body to enter another world. A whole new existence," he said quietly, "a whole new existence."

That's one of the few times he ever mentioned anything about heaven. He didn't talk much about hell, either. "We shouldn't be overly concerned about what heaven looks like or how hot hell is," Mr. Adams told me. "Our main concern should be the way we live while here on earth." I never will forget the way he looked at me when he said, "David, study the Bible. Discover for yourself what it means to have faith in God and in his Son, Jesus. Then, study the dictionary I gave you so that you can better share this faith with others."

I didn't speak. He looked at me and I looked at him. The silence we exchanged underlined what he had told me. Then, he closed the conversation by saying, "Trust in Jesus and pattern your life after his; take care of the way you act on earth. God will take care of you—forever."

The thing I remember most about Mr. Adams' funeral is the thought that kept going through my mind: "If Mr. Adams patterned his life after Jesus, then Jesus must really be something." And the thing that I remember most about Mr. Adams is that he, in his own words, " . . . took care of the way he acted." There's no doubt that God is taking care of him right now. It's like I said in the Christmas poem I wrote for him:

Some people celebrate Christmas once a year.
    This seems to please them.
Mr. Adams, you celebrate Christmas everyday.
    This must please God.
Thank you, Mr. Adams for all the gifts you have
    given me.
Thank you . . .

              for being interested in what I say
              and showing interest in what I
                 do.
Thank you . . .

              for believing in me
              and helping me to believe in my-
                 self.
Thank you . . .

              for being happy with me when
                 I am happy
              and being sad with me when I
                 am sad.
Thank you . . .

              for helping me when I need it
                 most
              and smiling at me when words
                 alone won't help.
Thank you . . .

              for telling me when I am wrong
              and praising me when I do right.

Thank you . . .

> for trying to understand me
> and helping me to understand
> myself.

Thank you most of all, Mr. Adams, *for you being
you.*